How
To
Tune-up
Your
Marriage For
Life

How To Tune-up Your Marriage For Life

Errol A. Bennett, D min.

To order additional copies of this book, contact:
Xlibris Corporation
1-888-795-4274
www.Xlibris.com
Orders@Xlibris.com
70073

TABLE OF CONTENTS

MARRIAGE TUNE-UP

Marriage is a marvelous institution designed by God. It is such an amazing thing when a man and a woman are joined together in holy matrimony as sanctioned by God. However, as lovely as it may be at the beginning of the marriage, if it is not given great attention and care it will suffer over time and eventually die. Like the vehicles that we drive and must maintain for good performance, our marriage needs to be maintained if we want it to last for life.

Every new vehicle comes with a manual which gives specific instructions on how to operate and maintain it for best performance. For optimum performance our vehicles must have regular maintenance. For every three months or six thousand kilometers the oil, lube and filter must be changed to keep the engine running well. The tires must be adequately inflated and rotated after so many thousand kilometers, and the wheels aligned for the most comfortable ride. With the proper maintenance and careful operation our vehicles will make it over all kind of roads, as well as through all kinds of weather.

If we can take so much interest in maintaining our vehicles which we only have for a short time, we should take more interest in our marriage which we have for a lifetime. Remember its, "til death do us part" when we get married.

Christians use the bible as their manual for marriage. It gives us all the instructions we need to have the most successful marriage in the world. The bible has laid down the proper foundations for all marriages. If couples would build their marriage on these foundations they would be better able to withstand the many storms their marriage will encounter. If we spend thousands of dollars to tune our pianos for better melody; tune our guitars for sweeter music; and tune our vehicles for better performance; why can't we spend money and time to tune up our marriages to get happiness for life? There are many reasons for marital break down; but if every married couple would take the time to evaluate their marriage regularly, then try to strengthen weak areas, and improve on strong areas: many marriages would not end in divorce.

** *IT'S TIME TO TUNE UP YOUR MARRIAGE: IT WILL WORTH THE TIME AND MONEY YOU PUT INTO IT.*

EXAMINE YOUR MARRIAGE

It is a good idea to examine our marriage whenever we find that we are not doing as well as when we just got married. Every marriage needs a frequent tune-up in order to do well and withstand the trials of life. There are a few specific areas that we cannot neglect if we want to have a happy and successful marriage. We must ask ourselves these important questions:

1. Love: Is my love for my spouse the same, stronger, or worse than when we just got married? If we are honest to ourselves we know deep inside how we feel about our mate.
2. Communication: Communication in a marriage is like the fuel we use in our vehicles. When the fuel lines are blocked it prevents the vehicle from running smoothly. The lines of communication can be damaged by years of negligence and misunderstanding. How is the line of communication between you at this time?
3. Sex: Sex is a wonderful gift given by God for married couples to enjoy. When sex is scarce or missing from the marriage; you know it is time for a tune up. The question is," Do we still make love as passionately as when we just got married?

Yes   No   Sometimes.

4. Mind: Our mind is a powerful tool, with it we control our whole being, and the way we think can affect our marriage. So are your thoughts for your mate as wonderful as when you just met? What do you think about yourself, and the role you play as a mate?
5. Romance: When you inspect your marriage, is romance a thing of the past, or you both still romancing each other? When was the last time you and your spouse spent some romantic time together?
6. Respect: Respect is vital for any marriage to survive the challenges of life. Isn't it funny how we will show respect to the boss, the mail person or any other person outside our marriage, but we disrespect our spouse, the person who should be closest to us. Do you have problem respecting each other?

7. Conflicts: Conflicts in marriage are inevitable, but the way they are resolved will determine our success in marriage. When there are too many conflicts, especially over trivial things, you know your marriage is in need of tuning. Do you find that these days you are having frequent unnecessary fights? Do you have a specific method of resolving conflicts?

8. Trust: Have you check your level of trust lately. One of the biggest complaint from couples is a lost of trust in the marriage. The level of trust that was there at the beginning has been lost over the years due to disappointments in one or both spouses. How is the level of trust now, high or low?

IN OUR MARRIAGE I WOULD LIKE TO:

1. Adjust:

2. Repair:

3. Replace

4. Restore

Marriage Tune-up

Check the foundation.

Every strong building has a deep and strong foundation; therefore every successful marriage must have a solid foundation. Many marriages failed because they were not built on strong foundations. Others failed because their foundations eroded due to years of spousal negligence. When we neglect our marriage, bit by bit the substance dries out of the relationship, until it eventually crumble.

As you look at these guidelines, it is for you to examine your life to see how well you are doing in your marriage. If you are not yet married, it is hope that you will learn how to avoid all the pitfalls of those marriages that have failed. Those of you who are married check to see if your contributions to your marriage have led to its success or failure. As a married couple you are both responsible to work hard to make your marriage happy and successful.

These are some points that you need to check as you examine your marriage.

Remember your first love

Remember your first love. Do you remember the first time you met? How you were *'so in love'*. The warm and fuzzy feelings you have for each other. Try to reflect on your days of courtship, and remember how the passion of your love was burning for your spouse. Think of all the things that triggered those sparks in your romance, try to focus on the times you spent together and how good you felt then. Your love for each other was so strong you believed that you could conquer any mountain or cross any river to be with each other. No one or nothing mattered then. You were seen as the **Love birds.** Remember the feelings that brought you into your marriage; and work hard to rekindle them. This is the first step in getting your marriage tuned.

Make dates with each other

It is understood that life is not as simple for you as it use to be at the beginning of your marriage. Things and time have changed; then you had more time to do many things, including spending more time with other. However, these days you are both busy with all the daily activities: job, children, household chores, meetings, and a host of other things. This leaves you with little time for yourself, let alone time for your spouse.

So to get your marriage back on track you need to make dates with each other again. Set aside time to spend with each other. This could be once per week, twice per month, or how ever often both of you can make it. Go out for walks, go see a movie, go for coffee or dinner. Get a babysitter and both of you just spend the time together alone. When possible, go away for a romantic weekend; try to relight the romantic fire. You may be on a tight budget so you may have to be real creative with your finance, but by all means both of you need to spend meaningful time with each other to make your marriage succeed.

Do not take each other for granted

One of the biggest complaints from married couples is that they often felt taken for granted by their spouse. This is from both parties, but wives are the ones who usually talk about the need to feel appreciated for even just being a wife to their husband. Do not take each other for granted. After years of marriage it is quite easy for married couples to take each other for granted. You need to pay attention, especially to the little things. Take time to compliment each other frequently. Practice it until it becomes a habit. Let your spouse know that you really appreciate everything; don't assume, say it from the heart.

Your Touch Means Much

Touch has great healing effect.It is true, we live on tight schedules; constantly running here and there. However, that should not prevent you from spending time in each other's arms. Your touch means a lot. It helps to keep the intimacy alive in your relationship, and it reassures your mate of your love. Both of you should develop a habit of touching each other frequently. This has nothing to do with sex per se, it just mean that you want to keep the fire burning between you. A hug, a holding of hands, a little kiss on the cheek, a pat on the back, a wink of the eye, any little touch that says 'I love you' will help to keep your love for each other growing.

Take Interest

Do you remember in courtship how you use to show interest in each other's activities. Even though you did not like wrestling you would watch it with him any way, or you did not like knitting but you hang out with her when she was knitting. Now things have changed, you lost interest in each other's hobbies. Now you complain about each other's hobbies or activities, instead of taking some interest and learning what the other is doing. To tune up your marriage, you need to take interest into what each other is doing. For example, if your spouse is interested in hockey you could try to understand a little about the game, you do not necessarily have to participate in the games, but by showing some interest, you help to keep the relationship strong. By showing no interest in what your spouse is doing could open the door for someone else to show interest, and this can lead to affairs.

Let's Talk Again

If your relationship is like others that I know; you will admit that during your courtship there was a lot of talking. You used to spend lots of time talking to each other, about everything under the sun and beyond. Then you wondered how you found so many things to talk about; especially if you were not the talkative one. But now you hardly talk anymore. This could be for any number of reasons; however, whatever may be the reason talking has become sparse you need to tune it up. Become friends again. Try to find things to talk about just like old times. There are many things in the world to talk about. Talk about current affairs, talk about life, talk about each other, focus on your feelings for each other and how both of you improve your relationship together. Be honest and open minded to each other, share your likes and dislikes in the marriage. Talk, talk, talk, it will help you to bring out many things that may be on your mind for a while. This is not a time to argue about anything, it's a time of sharing with each other.

Teamwork is a must

The day you got married you became one flesh. This means that even though you are two people with different feelings and opinions, you must work together as a team to make your marriage succeed. If you want your marriage to survive the pot holes and bumps on the road of life you must work together as a team. Both of you must take the responsibility to work on your marriage to make it succeed. You must share financial obligations, household duties, and everything that will help to lessen the stress in the marriage. Neither of you should feel burdened from being overworked because one spouse refuse to share the work. A frequent check with your spouse to see if both of you are still working toward the same goals will help to eliminate stress in your relationship.

Commitment

Commitment is a power packed word for all marriages to overcome trials and hardship. It may be time to review your commitment to each other. Take a look at your relationship and see if it is at the place that you want it to be. Your commitment to each other will help you to overcome the major hurdles of life. When was the last time you went down memory lane with commitment? By recommitting your life to each other and working hard your marriage will succeed. The reason many marriages failed is a lack of commitment from each partner to each other. Check to see if you have made any commitment with each over the years that were not fulfilled, and try to fulfill them.

Communications restored

Great communication is one of the vital signs of a healthy marriage; therefore, the line of communication must always be in good working order to keep the marriage alive. Talking is one way of expressing your thoughts and feelings to each other, so you should be able to talk freely to each other at all times. When there is a problem, talk to your spouse first before complaining to any one else. Most times when there is a problem between a couple they try to resolve it by talking to others rather than talking to their mate first. Words are more than just wind, they have power to build or destroy a relationship. That is the reason you must use your words wisely. The fire of many marriages has been extinguished by the unskillful use of words. Have you checked the wires of communications lately to see if they are working well, or have they been damaged or eroded by years of neglect? There are many reasons the wires of communication may have crossed, so cares must be taken at all times when trying to untangle the wires, so that you do not damage your marriage in the process. Communication is not only in words but also in actions as well, therefore, be careful of your actions. Do not say one thing and mean another. Remember, action speaks louder than words. So it is not always what we say but how we say it that affects our marriage.

Praises do wonders

Many spouses do not realize that the more they praise their mate the better their marriage will become. You must develop a habit of praising each other all the time. Praise each other for the skills, qualities, strengths, and talents you observed. Let your mate know how much these things have helped to improve your marriage. Praise helps to build self-esteem, and encourages your mate to work harder to make you happy. I know that this may be difficult for some people, depending on their background. Some people grew up not getting praises from others so they never learned the art of praise. However, with much practice you will be able to develop this habit. *Have you praise your mate lately?*

Understanding is vital

These are popular sayings in marriages "I don't understand you" and "You don't understand me" Do you feel that you have been misunderstood too many times and it is causing a problem? Check your lines of actions to see if it has been severed by your own self will. Understanding is a vital spark for a strong marriage, so it important you try to understand each other. Learn all you can about your mate. Try to discover the mood and temperament of each other. When you understand each other it makes it much easier for your marriage to run smoothly. You must be willing to give and take in everything. Try to put yourself in your mate's shoes and see if you can figure out why things happened. Be realistic at all. *It's times Revitalize understanding.*

What about acceptance ?

Many couples struggle in their marriage because they try to change their mates. Believe it or not there are some things in our mates that we just have to accept and learn to tolerate. The truth is if the thing(s) that you want to change were there and you did not address them during courtship, it makes it difficult to expect changes later on in your marriage. Sometimes it is even unreasonable to expect changes because you did not address them earlier in your marriage. Try to rekindle the fire of acceptance. Show the same tolerance now as you did when you were dating. Remember that you accepted your mate with all the faults and *failures, therefore, learn to accept the things that neither of you can change.*

Get Rid of Resentments

Resentment is a killer. Many marriages died because couples developed resentments for each other over a long time. When there are unresolved issues it caused resentments that slowly grew inside each spouse. Those resentments prevent your marriage from reaching its greatest potentials. For example, one spouse may resent the way the other spouse spend money, and after speaking about it and see no change in behavior, a resentment may develop for that spouse. Try to get rid of resentment because it will kill your love, your mood, your desire, your motivation, your sex life, and drain you emotionally: then eventually kill your marriage.

Always try to keep promises

One of the things that can destroy a marriage is broken promises.

Promises broken are worse than promises not made. Two many broken promises will destroy the relationship between you and your spouse. Try not to make promises you cannot fulfill. And if you do make a promise and you find you cannot fulfill it, apologize, and make alternative plans. Keeping your promises will help to keep trust alive in your marriage. If **you have not been able to keep your** promises, now **is the time to begin as a way of tuning your marriage.**

Show Appreciation

There are many spouses who do not know how to show appreciation to one another. Some couples have lived together for years, yet they would not even let their mates know that they have been appreciated for who they are, and for the things that they have done. Try to show appreciation to each other everyday. Do not wait until something happened before you try to say nice things about your **mate. Showing appreciation to your spouse will help to smooth the rough edges of your marriage.**

Be Sincere

It is much harder to be phony than to be sincere, because you constantly have to cover up when you are phony. Make it your business to be sincere to each other in everything. When you are sincere you have nothing to fear, and your relationship will flourish every day. Look **inside yourself and see if you have been sincere to your self or to your spouse**. If that **has not been the case then you need to change it now to make it better for both of you.**

How generous are you ?

Generosity is a good spark for a successful marriage. The more you give the more you will receive. Give lots of love, give lots of kind words, give lots of your time, give lots of yourself, give lots of gifts, give lots of everything to each other and you will get it back in return. This is not a one way street, each spouse must make the effort to give to each other, especially the things that your spouse needs most to give your marriage stability. If your spouse **needs lots of love, then give lots of love and watch your marriage grow.**

Intimacy

It is time to check the degree of intimacy between you and your spouse. Are you keeping in close contact with each other? Remember, intimacy is not only for the bedroom. The touches, the smiles, the eye contacts, the little kisses throughout the day will help to heighten the pleasure of lovemaking. Keep in mind **that you have become one flesh and nothing should come between you. Try to keep the level of intimacy high at all times to prevent outside** interference. Intimacy **is not only to fulfill sexual** needs. but **also to keep you together forever. It is the glue that keeps the relationship tightly knitted together.**

A Cry for Passion

Many marriages have suffered from lack of passion, and it is hoped that yours is not one of them. Do you consider yourself a passionate mate? When you are passionate to your mate you create an atmosphere for your mate to feel relaxed knowing that you are there and that you care? Take time to be passionate to each other, it will strengthen your relationship. **Each spouse must work hard to keep the passion burning in your marriage, then there will be no lacking for passion.**

Courtship Review

When was the last time you review your courtship days? It is a good practice for both of you to spend some time together reflecting on the fun days of your courtship. This should bring back some pleasant memories that will help to remind you of the reasons that you got married. Those days you felt like were lovers; nothing or no one could have come between you. You were hot items: you found ways to make each other happy, and you felt like you belong to each other. Yes, time has changed since then; there is a lot of responsibilities now, and it seems as if there is no way **out. However, as you review those loving days of courtship, talk about ways how both of you can rekindle the fire in your relationship and your marriage and keep the fire burning for a long, long time.**

Little Things that Count

Every good marriage is built up *of "little things". The* little things will be remembered for a lifetime, whether they are pleasant or unpleasant. As you tune-up your marriage you need to think about those little things that will help to improve your marriage. The little love notes, little surprise parties, little dinner dates, little bunches of flowers, little planned getaways, little breakfasts in bed, and any little thing that you can think of that would put a big smile on your spouse's face will help to boost your marriage. Since marriage is a give and take institution, it requires both parties to get involved for it to succeed. There **needs not be a particular reason; just do it, because you love each other.**

Romance in Marriage

Romance is not only for courtship; it is for a lifetime of marriage. Romance should not stop now that you are married. As a matter of fact romance between you must become more intense now that you have the love of your life in your care. Keep on saying those sweet and kind words to each other as you did before you were married. Tease your mate with those nice sexy outfits. Dress up for each other sometimes. Husbands, buy your wives nice sexy under wears and lingerie. Wives, be sure to wear sexy under wears for your husbands. Let your mate know that you are madly in love. Do not be afraid to let your mate know that you are in the mood for loving. Talk like adults show your mate signs of wanting to be desired. Make up a romantic name for each other and use it often. A **marriage without romance is like a car without battery.**

Have Confidence

Having confidence in yourself as well as in your spouse will help your marriage to overcome many humps in life. High self-esteem is important in helping to build confidence in each other. However, a spouse with low self-esteem will put little effort in building the marriage. That is the reason both of you must guard against doing or saying anything that would promote low self-esteem, and hinder self confidence. Build each other's confidence with praises and compliments. Do not talk down to your spouse, it creates an atmosphere for low self-esteem, and kills one's confidence. If you are having problems with low self-esteem it is best to seek professional help for the sake of your marriage. Do **not be afraid to discuss your lack of confidence with your spouse, because that in it self should boost your confidence, as your spouse try to offer lots of support in building your confidence.**

Bring back the Trust

Trust is one of the ingredients found in the foundation of marriage. Take away trust and your marriage is empty and dry like a car without gas. Look at the trust between you and your spouse, and see if it is at the level you want it to be. If it not then you and your spouse need to examine your relationship to see where the break down happened. Many times lack of trust is caused by misunderstanding, or it may be damaged by years of emotional or psychological abuse. Once you discover the reason for the break down, both of you need to spend some time repairing it. **Damaged trust is like a punctured car, you cannot get too far with it. The tires must be repaired before you can move on. Repairing trust in your spouse may take a long time, depending on the circumstances, but with a willing mind and good effort it can be *done. It takes two to pull through, so work hard to make it happen so that you can move on with your life.***

When trust in your spouse has been lost you must allow yourself to look beyond faults, otherwise it will hold you back. Try to change your own attitude toward your spouse as long as there is genuine change in behavior. There are times when the marriage is held hostage because one spouse refuse to release the other of the "offence" committed. In order to get your marriage tuned and ready for life, you must build back trust in your spouse.

Learning from each other

Marriage is a great institution with a lifetime of lessons to learn from each other. It truly will take a life time to learn every thing about your mate. One of the great discoveries in marriage is that we learn something new about our mate every day. Every incident in our life should teach us a lesson if we are willing to learn. Therefore, as a couple you should develop the habit of learning something from each other all the time. Study your spouse as an individual. Try to understand your spouse's personality, and personal needs. That is how you will know when it is the best time to approach your spouse about certain issues. **Do not allow pride to prevent you from learning valuable lessons from your spouse; the lessons you learn today could save your marriage later.**

Take pride in your Marriage

To be married is such a wonderful thing. It is such a great feeling to know that of all the people in the world you two have been brought together to share in this oneness called marriage. As a married couple you are different from all the other couples in the world. No two persons in this world are alike, and that's the same for couples; therefore you should take pride in your marriage. Be proud of yourself, and of the person you married. Let your spouse and others know how you feel about your mate. Hi light the good qualities and talents of your spouse, after all there must be some good things that brought you together. If there are **reasons for you not to feel proud about your marriage, discuss them and try to work together to make it succeed.**

Put away Assumptions

Assumptions will destroy the relationship between you and your spouse. When we assume we hurt ourselves and the ones we love. When assumptions turned out to be false it put a strain on our relationships. As a couple you should try to live so that you have a clear knowledge of each other. When you know your mate well it makes it easier to deal with various issues in your marriage without having to assume anything. Put **away assumptions and generalizations and replace them with facts. Get the facts from your spouse; not from other sources.**

Get rid of Corrosions

There are some marriages that are on the verge of collapse due to years of corrosions from anger, malice, and strife that they have endured. Anger, malice and strife should not be a part of any one's life. If you or your spouse suffers from any of these deadly poisons, you should get rid of them as quickly as possible, by replacing them with **love and affection.** In order to tune your marriage properly you must each work on your own life to get rid of these things. Anger has a way of preventing us from enjoying our own life, which also prevents us from enjoying a relationship with others, especially the ones we truly love. Some spouses may have to get professional help to manager their anger, but if that's what it takes to save your marriage, then don't be ashamed get help.

Change The Beat

Like everything else in our lives our marriage can become dull sometimes. Whenever you notice that things in your marriage have become a routine, it is time to change your beat. Try a little tenderness sometimes. Do something unusual to change the dull scene. Make the sacrifice to spend more uninterrupted time with each other. Both of you can work to change the beat, or do it as a surprise to each other. Be creative, keep changing the beat.

Be an Optimist

It is much easier to see all the negative things in life, than all the positives that happened.It is easier to see all the faults in your spouse, than the good things they have done. It is much easier to complain about the burnt roast, rather than to give compliment for the effort made in preparing delicious roast. Be an optimist try to see the bright side of things with your spouse, even though others may not agree with you. Being optimistic will help your mate's confidence. Dream the same dreams and you will go to the highest height together. Try to use the unpleasant situations in your marriage to your advantage. Your mind is a very powerful tool; use it to change the negatives into positives. Criticize constructively not destructively.

Adjust Your Listening Skills

Men and women express themselves differently; therefore it is important that husbands, especially become good listeners. Listen with your whole being: your ears for the tone of voice, your eyes watching for facial expressions of any kind of hidden messages. What comes from the lips may not be the true message of the heart ;but with good listening skills you will know that something is wrong. Your spouse is not a mind reader; therefore you must be honest with each other when sharing your feelings. **When you are honest about your true feelings there will be no need for your spouse to decode any hidden messages.**

Companionship a must

Companionship is a must for your marriage to stay on the right track. Companionship means that both of you become best fiiends.It means that both of you are going to spend lots of time together, because the more time you spend together the better you will get to understand each other. When you do things together it will also help to make your relationship better. **Becoming** best friends will eliminate the need to complain to a third party when something goes wrong between you.

Cherish each other daily

Everyone in this world is precious. However, to become one with another human being is so amazing; therefore should not be taken lightly. You must cherish each other daily. You should see each other as a rare precious gem and treat each other as such. Do not take your spouse for granted. The same qualities that brought you together should motivate you to treasure your mate. When you treasure your mate you treat him/her with special care. The **more you cherish your mate the brighter both of you will shine.**

Review Your Expectations

When you got married there were many written and unwritten expectations from each of you. Many of those expectations may have been met, while unfortunately others fell out by the wayside. It is time for both of you to take a look at your lives together and review all those expectations and where you are with them. There may have been disappointments, road blocks, or other obstacles in the way, but now you have to work hard to meet future expectations.

Disagreements Inevitable

Disagreements and arguments are inevitable in marriages, but the way we deal with them will make the difference in our happiness. You will not always agree with each other, but you must learn to respect each other's opinions, especially those that are quite different from what you believe. In all cases try to avoid confrontations before friends, your children, and other family members. Do not try to humiliate your spouse at anytime. When there is an argument, if it is at all possible use the bedroom to solve them. Pillow talk will solve more problems than all yelling and shouting. Study the mood of your mate and figure out the best time to discuss certain issues. Use **wisdom at all times when trying to resolve problems.It would be a good idea not to talk about delicate issues when either of you is tired or angry.**

Responsibilities

Is your marriage showing signs of lack of responsibilities? Talk about it. Both of you need to take responsibility for your own actions. Try not to pass the blame to someone else. This often happens when one does not want to be held accountable for anything. Whenever a mistake is made; admit it, apologize and move on. Remember **that you are both adults and you should act as such.**

Respect

Respect is another key ingredient in a healthy marriage. Respect is one of those **'little'** things that slip away from us over the years. There is the tendency for spouse to treat everyone else with certain respect except your own spouse. For some couples the respect factor just went through the window over the years. However; the same degree of respect that was given from the beginning must continue to the end. Review your level of respect daily, and repair any broken areas that you discover. Each **of you is expected to maintain the behavior that will earn the utmost respect from each other.**

Forgiveness (Forgive what?)

Forgiveness is not a word used often in many marriages. Many marriages ended in divorce because one spouse would not forgive. Everybody makes mistakes, it does not matter who we are, so we must learn to forgive one another. Do **unto others the same things you want them to do unto you. If you want forgiveness then you must practice forgiving** others. Forgiveness will help to maintain a positive relationship in your marriage. Do not hold grudges. Forgiveness means that the mistake is erased and you are willing to try again. Try not to dwell on the past. When you have an argument about something, deal with the current issue. Do not bring the issue of what happened last month, unless it has a direct bearing on the subject. Many spouses will use old issues to stir up arguments. When this happens you know that you were not forgiven for the mistakes you made. You know yourself: **look inside your heart and see if you are a forgiving person.**

Patience is valuable

Patience is a virtue that will help you to slowly get over those humps in your marriage. Patience does not happen overnight, you may have to work hard to develop your patience. You must learn to be patient with each other. Do not allow impatience to ruin your marriage; try to increase your patience daily. When you have patience both of you will be able to wait out the turbulence in your marriage. With patience you will not be quick to throw in the towel, but you will be willing to hold on for the light **of day. Heartaches will come, and** there will be some hurts, but with understanding, hard work, and patience healing will come eventually.

Creativity

It is said that variety is the spice of life. This is important for your marriage as well as any other parts of your life. Do not allow your marriage to suffer boredom due to the lack of creativity. Both of you are responsible to find ways to keep the fire burning in your marriage. Some spouses like to blame one another for the boredom they experience in their marriage; but if each of you would work hard to create a wonderful marriage, there would be no need for boredom. Be spontaneous, surprise each other with different plans, especially things that both of you like to **do. When you are in love with other it is quite easy for both of you to find fun things to do together that will brighten your marriage.**

Setting Priorities

Setting priorities and living by them will help to maintain stability in your life. When you set priorities you will eliminate many obstacles that would prevent your relationship from growing successfully. Many marriages suffer because one or both spouses do not know how to set priorities. Set short-term and long-term goals for yourself and for your marriage and work hard to achieve them. You will not reach all the goals you set in life; however, it will be of great help if you get your priorities straight, when you set your goals. Know how to place the people and things in your life in their proper place.lt **is time to review your priorities to see if they are where you want them to be.**

When was the last time you had a good laugh ?

Do you remember how you use to laugh together? So what happened? Your busy schedules may have prevented you from finding time to spend together to laugh. Take time to re-connect. Review your relationship and try to get back on track, so both of you can get back that closeness. You used to laugh at any and everything; now all that has changed. Laughter will do great wonders for you and your marriage, so go ahead surprise yourself. Try to find something to laugh about, even a joke from the comic strip. If laughter is the best medicine, then use it to cure all those hurts in your life and in your marriage.

Warning Signals

Divorce does not 'just happened' it usually comes after many warning signals have been ignored. Do not take anything for granted. Pay attention to your partner. Know what is happening in your spouse's life. Whenever you notice that everything is not as it use to be, it is time to find out what went wrong. Review your feelings with each other regularly, and be honest with each other. Do not say "everything is fine," when you know deep within you something is wrong. As a couple, neither of you has the right to neglect each other. Look out for the best interest of your spouse. Try to work out your problems as soon as they come and do not allow them to build up; they may lead to marriage break **down. Tune-up any area of your marriage that you notice is getting loose.**

Say No to Routines

Marriages can be destroyed by routines if you are not careful. When it seems like everything has become a routine in your marriage, it is time to dust off your wedding album or videos, and review them together. Reflect on that special day when you got married. Take the time to recapture those wonderful moments you had together when you just got married. Refresh your memories of the reasons got married. Talk about your first kiss, and all the things you love about each other. If it is possible, plan a trip to the place where you had your honeymoon, and try to rekindle the fire. Make **every effort to avoid getting in a routine in your marriage, it will tear you apart.**

Be Polite to Each Other

It is quite easy for you to become impolite to each other, especially when you are angry or in a bad mood. Be polite to each other at all times. Do not forget that you have become one flesh; therefore as you would like to be treated so you must treat your mate. Be wise in your selection of words. Think about your spouse's feelings before you speak. Words can be very damaging when not used properly. Please **and Thank you are always appropriate, even though you may be angry with your spouse.**

Anticipation

Anticipation will help to keep the sparks burning in your marriage. Everybody has a certain level of anticipation in him/her. You must anticipate the good times as well as the bad times, and prepare yourself for both of them.

Be vigilant, always looking out for the signs of good or bad times, and learn how to deal with them when they come. Anticipation does not have to be negative, it must be in a positive mode always. Anticipation will help you to get over the difficult spots in your marriage.

Protect your Investment

Remember that your marriage is a lifetime investment in each other; therefore you must make great efforts to get the best return on your investment. You must cherish each other better than any rubies or gold. Be sure to let your spouse feel precious. When your spouse knows how you feel, there will be no need for nagging.

Fantasize about Who ?

Fantasize about your mate, and let your mate know that you are hungry for romance.It takes less energy to have an affair with your mate than with someone else. Don't be afraid to let your spouse know what you are thinking about him/her. Some wives would be happy to hear that they are sexy from their husbands, than from someone else. Use your imaginations to help you dispel boredom from your marriage. Your fantasies do not have to be out of the norm, or against your partner's wishes; but wonderful fantasies that will help to enhance your marriage.

Do not Compare

Never try to compare your mate with anyone else, albeit past lovers, your friends, your friend's mate, your mate's friend, or your friend's friend. This will lead to jealousy, nagging, and resentment. Both of you may have your faults and failures, but you must treat each other with the greatest love for each other.

Are You a Complement ?

When you got married it was two people from two different worlds coming together as one. However, these days you may not feel like you are a part of each other. You should try to be the best for your spouse. Try to pick up the pieces in your daily living. You must work hard together as a team to fight the challenges in your life. You are one flesh behave as one.

Decisions. Decisions

Decision making is a part of our daily lives. As a couple you make decisions as an individual and as a team. Whenever you make major decisions it needs full cooperation from both of you. Both of you do not always have to agree, but you must learn to compromise at times to achieve the best results for everyone involved. When you can't see eye to eye on decisions, try to take a look at each decision from all angles, and not just from your point of view. Make sure both of you understand how the decisions will affect or benefit the family. Major decisions require wisdom and understanding.

Negligence

Checking, checking : Many marriages suffer great turbulence due to negligence. You must make sure that neither of you neglect each other's needs. Do not neglect the care of yourself or the care of your mate. You must take care of your hygiene, your clothes, your health, and all areas of your life that bring stability and happiness to your marriage. It is important that you remember your vows to each other, and focus on the reasons you got married. Do not neglect your duties and your responsibilities, because when you do your marriage will be in trouble. Take **a good look at your marriage and see if you are doing the things that are required to make it succeed.**

Review Your Goals

In order to keep your marriage above the waters you must take time out of your busy schedules to review your lives together.

A. *Keep updating your personal and marital goals.*
B. *Check your long–term and short–term goals,*
C. *Get rid of any inferiority complex that you may have.*
D. *Check your communication lines regularly.*
E. *Change your creativity skills, improve on old ones.*
F. *Inspect marriage compass; see if both of you are going in the same direction.*
G. *Take a look at the temperature to see if it is at the right degree. Are you able to control temper?*
H. *How is your relationship? Is there intimacy between you?*
I. *Is your love for each other still fully charged?*
J. *Are the sparks still flying in your sex life?*
K. *Is the light of respect, wisdom and understanding burning bright in your life?*

Adaptability

Adaptability is significant for your marriage. Being adaptable will help both of you to deal with changes in your marriage. Both of you must be willing to adapt to each other's personality, and all other changes that you will face from time to time. Your love for each other will make it quite easy to make any change in your marriage without either of you getting **hurt. Adaptability may come with compromise, but it should not infringe on your rights.**

Friendship

Friendship is a must for all successful marriages. Some couples are man and wife, but find it difficult to become best of friends. Best friends share everything, and find it a pleasure to be together all the time. You tell your best friend secrets. Your best friend knows all about you. You try hard not to hurt your friends and there is certain amount of respect you give to your friends, which some time is missing from marriages. Are **you your spouse's best friend? Can your spouse tell you ANYTHING without feeling being judged? If you are not, you need to be find out from your spouse what needs to change so that you two can become best of friends.**

Reality check

As in everything else, marriage is for real. Both of you must be realistic about everything pertaining to your marriage. From the moment you got married you must face the facts of living with each other, regardless of faults or failures. However, it is true that if both of you do not work hard on your relationship your marriage will fail. It is a reality that both of you should try to live within your means, otherwise you will always be in debt. Many marriages failed because one or both spouses refuse to accept some of the realities of life. The fact is that there are things in your own live, or the life of your mate that you may not be able to change; therefore, you will have to accept them as they are and live with them. **Every now and again both of you must check to make sure that you are on the same level of reality. Because sometimes we can set our expectations higher than we can reach them and that create a problem for your marriage.**

Lying is not acceptable !

Lying is one of the most destructive things to any marriage. Lying shows a lack of trust in yourself and in your mate. If you have been lying to your spouse then it is time to change. Tell the truth always. When you tell the truth you do have to worry about being found out. Lying comes in various forms: by not expressing your true feelings to each other, you are actually lying to your spouse. For example, if your spouse did something that hurt you, but instead of stating your true feelings, you act as if you are alright yet deep inside you are hurting, you are both lying to your spouse and to yourself. Whenever the wife fake orgasms, she is in fact lying to her husband, as well as her own body. Check **your life to make sure that you're not lying to each other. A tuned marriage is free from all forms of lying.**

Get Rid of Gaps

Every little gap that is left unattended has the potential to become a gulf in your marriage. Every time you allow something to come between you it widens the gap in your relationship. Try to take care of the little problems as soon as they occur so that they would not lead to bigger problems. Take **a look at your relationship to see if there are gaps, and if there are gaps, try to get rid of them. Your marriage will grow successfully.**

No Doldrums

Every marriage has the potentials for doldrums, but your strong love for each other will help you to endure them. Look out for them and be prepared to deal with them early. Be creative in dealing with doldrums; the more creative you are, the better you will be able to handle **them. Look out for each other, and try to help each other through these difficult times. Please remember that you are both responsible for your own actions so you can choose to deal the doldrums in your marriage or you can stand back and watch it fall apart.**

Spice-up your sex life

I can remember the many times our cooking got burnt because we were too busy doing 'other things' leaving the cooking unattended. It is said that **variety is the spice of life.** This is so true when it comes to sex. It does not matter if you are married for six months or sixty years, you must find a way to keep sex pleasurable between you. We know that the bedroom is the ideal place in the house to make love. However, in reality when two lovers are together any part of the house is **ideal.** The kitchen, the living room, laundry room, (on the spin cycle) attic, bath room; any where that is safe will do.

Do you remember how you couldn't keep your hands off each other? So what happened? Now is the time to bring back the spice in sex. Since we are so busy we have to change the way we take care of sex in our marriage. Sex with your mate can be at any time as long as both of you agreed. It can be for two minutes or for two hours. Since your life is so busy, the one area of your life that you must take time for is your sex life. You and your spouse must have a plan for sex.

Sex is a very important part of a successful marriage. Sex is sacred and was designed by God for pleasure as well for procreation. Many marriages failed due to ignorance about sex. Lack of communication in sex is one of the biggest problems facing many married couples. Many couples find it much easier to have sex, than to even have a good conversation about it. Depending on one's culture and background, sex may have been thought of as something unpleasant to talk about. Some people received wrong teaching about sex, so they do not have the proper knowledge about it. Therefore when they get married they don't really know what to do. The key for success is talk, talk, talk, and more talk about your sex life with your mate. Honesty is the best policy if you want to improve on your sex life. Too many couples are suffering because of dishonesty. They fail to share their true feelings with each other which eventually lead to a break down in their marriage.

With so much information on sex today there should be no excuse for a lousy sex life. Get as much facts as you can on the subject. Study, study, study the successful sex life of other couples. Be creative! Spice up your own sex life. There is a big difference between sex and love making. Any couple can have sex when they get together, but love making goes beyond that. It begins in the mind then transferred to the rest of the body. Sex does not just happen, especially for some ladies. This means that both of you should be thinking about each other all the time. Send each other text messages, emails, notes, anything that will trigger sex in the brains. Then when you get together to make love do not allow other things to cloud your mind. Your mind must be free to concentrate on your mate when making love. This is not the time to be thinking about the bills, or any other thing that may have occurred during the day. When you are making love it is a time to give and receive pleasure; therefore there should be no time to think of anything else. Many relationships break down when one or both partners are not sexually satisfied.

There are many stories about wives faking orgasms; tying to fool their husbands making them believe that they are enjoying sex with them. That is not right. That is a deception, and wives who do such thing are not only lying to their husbands, but deceiving themselves. Do not forget that the whole idea of lovemaking is to give pleasure to each other. If you are not being sexually satisfied it your responsibility to talk to your spouse about it. That is why you need to become best friends and lovers, and not only husband and wife. This is where good communication in your marriage is important, because instead of pretending that you are enjoying sex, you would discuss ways of making it better with your spouse. If you cannot resolve the sexual problem between you then both of you should get good counseling. You should also research the subject, and do all you can to make sex pleasurable. True **love means doing all you can to have a happy** marriage.

You should develop a comfort zone in your relationship where both of you are feeling comfortable to shed your inhibitions so you can talk freely to each other about your sexual feelings. Your likes and dislikes, your desires and needs. This is also the time to tell your spouse of anything you know that is truly killing your sex life. For example: poor hygiene; smelly socks; bad breath; not having regular showers, and so on. Sex **is a wonderful thing. For many couples this is their recreation time. With all the numerous benefits that sex offers it's surprising that married couples don't make the time to have more sex.** If you have found that your sex life is not as it use to be due to lack of interest you and your spouse need to talk. Use wisdom in tuning up your sex life and your marriage.

Marriage Tune-up

Marriage

M—Motivation: As partners we are motivated to work hard to make our marriage succeed. Without motivation we will quit when trials and hardship come. Each of us must give 100 percent effort to make our marriage successful.

A—Attention: Our undivided attention to each other will keep us together, and prevent others from coming between us. We must take time to compliment each other for the "little things" we do to make each other happy.

R—Respect: "Give it and it shall be returned to you" will be the motto for respect in our marriage. Respect will be given without reservation, regardless of our faults and failures. We will try to use kind words to each other as much as possible.

R—Relationship: A good and healthy relationship will keep the fire burning in our marriage. We will rely on each other for support just like the members of our own body; knowing that we became one flesh when we got married.

I—Individuality: We acknowledge the fact that we are two individuals with two different personalities, coming together as one, yet maintaining our individuality. We must accept each other for our own unique personality and try to live with the differences.

A—Accord: "Can two walk together except they agree" Amos 3:3. We must be on one accord in order to overcome the trials in our life. We will try to operate on the same wave length at all times to make our marriage succeed.

G—God: God is the master designer of all marriages; therefore He should be head and chief engineer of our marriage. He must lead us in all our plans, and we must rely on Him to fix all broken parts of our marriage.

E—Endless Love: Our love had a beginning, but with our commitment to each other, and with God's help it shall not have an ending. Our love is the glue that will help us to withstand all the storms we will face in life.

How to solve Conflicts

Every marriage will encounter some kind of conflicts at one time or another and the way these conflicts are resolved will determine the success of your marriage. Here are tips to guide you when dealing with conflicts with your spouse.

When conflicts come:

A. Asses the situation carefully.
B. Think before you speak—words are powerful, and can be quite damaging if not used appropriately. Do not say anything that you might regret later on.It does not matter how many times you apologized, a word wrongly spoken will last for a long time.
C. Do not criticize or name-call, this will only make the conflict worse.
D. Be thoughtful, think of your mate's feelings too.
E. Do not blame anyone or anything; accept responsibility for your own actions or behaviors.
F. Do not generalize-stick to the present issues and deal with them as they are.
G. Speak calmly and rationally. If you are too angry to speak, say so and take a time-out until you feel you are ready to deal with the issues rationally. Do **not use time-out as a means of avoiding the matters. Do make it a point to resume the conversation after you are calm.**
H. Listen carefully and show respect at all times. There must be a reason things got to this in the first place. Listen not only with your ears, but with your whole being.
I. Be fair; if you are wrong admit it, and try to work out a resolution.
J. Leave room for negotiation.
K. Deal with the immediate issues, not past issues unless they are relevant to the present one.
L. When tempers get too hot, take some time to cool off before resuming discussion. Go for a walk, listen to music, talk to yourself.
M. Put yourself in your mate's place.
N. Do not hold grudges-when **it's over, its over: kiss and make up.**

O. Do not assume anything, ask questions about things you do not understand, your spouse is obligated to give you an honest answer

P. When arguing, avoid phrases such as: **"You always . . ."** **"You never . . ."**

Q. Stick to the point and make it short, same day delivery is the best, it avoids left over Baggage, that can become a mountain of problems.

R. Seek to end your conflicts with a sincere apology.

S. Even though you may be angry with each other, try not to sleep in separate rooms or in separate beds. This will put a wedge between you and delay the process of resolution. The longer it takes to resolve conflicts. the wider the gap will become in your relationship: therefore it is best to always try for an early resolution. Conflicts **are not always easy to resolve, but your love for each other should help you to overcome those difficult times. Tune up all those areas that have been bothering you all along.**

The Christian

"couple"

MARRIAGE TUNE-UP

The Christian Couple

The Bible has given us a clear view of the way each Christian should live in order to maintain a good relationship with one another on earth, before we can have a good relationship with Jesus Christ. John 4:20 says," If a man say, I love God, and hates his brother, he is a liar: for he that loves not his brother whom he hath seen, how can he love God whom he hath not seen?

This is the message for all Christian married couples, because there are Christian couples who believe that they can fight like cats and dogs, and have hatred in their hearts, yet say they love God. **Colossians 3:8-9 remind us to:**

Put off the old man with all these:

1. Anger.
2. Wrath.
3. Malice.
4. Blasphemy.
5. Filthy communication out of your mouth.
6. Lie not one to another.

Put on therefore;

1. Bowels of mercies.
2. Kindness.
3. Humbleness of mind.
4. Meekness.
5. Longsuffering.
6. Forbearing one another.
7. Forgiving one another.
8. Charity.
9. Peace of God.
10. Be thankful.

** Let the word of Christ dwell in you richly in all wisdom.
** Teach and admonish one another in psalms and hymns and spiritual songs.
** Whatsoever ye do, do all in the name of the Lord Jesus.

1 Peter 3. Peter emphasized the fact that Christian couples must learn to live together as one, and be happy. This is how he put it:

1. Be harmonious.
2. Be sympathetic.
3. Show brotherly love.
4. Be kindhearted
5. Be humble in spirit.
6. Do not render evil for evil.
7. Do not render insult for insult.
8. Learn to give each other blessings.
9. Have the same purpose in mind.
10. Study God's word together.

It is very important that all Christian couples follow the instructions God gives us in His words if they want to have a great marriage. Many marriages suffer because of ignorance; others fail because people refuse to live by the principles in God's words. The Bible shows us how to communicate with each other in every aspect of our lives, and if we practice these simple rules to our lives, our lives would be happier, whether we are single or married. This is what the Bible says about using words, using our tongues, and keeping silent at times.

Kind Words

Job 4:4-Thy words have upheld him that was stumbling, and thou hast strengthened the feeble knees.

Prov. 15:1~A soft answer turns away wrath: but a harsh word stirs up anger.

Prov. 25:15—By long forbearing is a ruler persuaded, and a gentle tongue breaks a bone.

Prov. 31:26~She opens her mouth with wisdom, and on her tongue is the law of kindness.

Isa. 50:4—The Lord God has given me the tongue of the learned, that I should know how to speak a word in season to him that is weary: he awakens me morning by morning, he wakens mine ear to hear as the learned.

Know When to Keep Silent

Ecc. 3:7A time to tear, and a time to sew; a time to keep silence and a time to speak.

Prov. 17:27~He who has knowledge spares his words: and a man of understanding is of a calm spirit.

Matt. 5:37—But let your' Yes' be 'Yes' and your 'No', 'No'. For whatsoever is more than these is from the evil one.

Watch how you speak

Col. 4:6~ Let your speech be always with grace, seasoned with salt, that you may know how ye ought to answer each one.

James 3: 2—For we all stumble in many things. If any one does not stumble in word the same is a perfect man, able also to bridle the whole body.

Speak No Evil

Eph. 4:31—Let all bitterness, wrath, anger, and clamor, and evil speaking, be put away from you, with all malice.

James 4:11—Do not speak evil one of one another, brethren. He who speaks evil of his brother, speaks evil of the law and judges the law . . .

1 Peter 2: 1 Therefore, lay aside all malice, and all deceit, hypocrisy, envy, and all evil speaking.

1 Peter 3:10—For he who would love life, and see good days, let him refrain his tongue from evil, and his lips from speaking deceit.

Control your tongue-Save your Marriage

James 3:6—And the tongue is a fire, a world of iniquity. The tongue is so set among our members that it defiles the whole body, and sets on fire the course of nature; and it is set on fire by hell.

Psalm 34:10—Keep thy tongue from evil, and thy lips from speaking guile.

Prov. 13:3~He that keeps his mouth keeps his life; but he that opens wide his lips shall have destruction.

Prov. 21:23~Whoso keeps his mouth and his tongue, keeps his soul from troubles.

Self-Control

Prov. 16:32~He that is slow to anger is better than the mighty; and he that rules his spirit than he that takes a city.

Prov. 17:28—Even a fool is counted wise when he holds his peace. When he shuts his lips, he is considered perceptive.

Prov. 25:28-He that hath no rule over his own spirit is like a city that is broken down, and without walls.

God's Expectations of Husbands

Gen.2:24~ Therefore shall a man leave his father and his mother, and shall cleave unto his wife: and they shall be one flesh.

Deut. 24:5—When a man has taken a new wife, he shall not go out to war, neither shall he be charged with any business: but he shall be free at home one year, and bring happiness to his wife which he hath taken.

Prov. 5:18—Let thy fountain be blessed: and rejoice with the wife of thy youth

Ecc. 9:9—Live joyfully with the wife whom you love all the days of the life of vain life.

Mark 10: 9 Therefore what God has joined together, let no man separate.

Eph. 5:25 Husbands, love your wives, even as Christ also loved the church, and gave himself for it.

1 Peter 3:7 Likewise, ye husbands, dwell with them according to knowledge, giving honor unto the wife, as unto the weaker vessel, and as being heirs together of the grace of life; that your prayer may not be hindered.

Colossians 3:19—Husbands, love your wives and be not bitter against them. 1 Peter 3:7—Honor your wife—treat her with dignity.

God's expectations for Wives

Prov. 11:16 A gracious woman retains honor; and strong men retain riches.

Prov. 12:4 An excellent wife is the crown to her husband: but she who causes shame is like rottenness in his bones.

Prov. 14:1 Every wise woman builds her house; but the foolish pulls it down with her hands.

Prov. 31:10 Who can find a virtuous woman? for her worth is far above rubies.

Prov. 31:30 Favor is deceitful, and beauty is vain: but a woman that fears the Lord, she shall be praised.

Prov. 18:2 He who finds a wife finds a good thing, and obtains favor from the Lord.
Prov. 19:14 House and riches are the inheritance of fathers; and a prudent wife is from the Lord.

Prov. 31:11—The heart of her husband doth safely trust in her, so that he shall have no need of spoil.

Eph. 5:22—Wives submit yourselves unto your own husbands, as unto the Lord.

1 Tim. 3:11—Even so must wives be grave, not slanderers, sober, faithful in all things.

Titus 2:4-5~Be sober* love their husbands * love their children * be discreet (sensible) * chaste (pure) * keeper at home (workers at home) * good (kind) * obedient to their own husband. *1 Peter 3:1.*

God's expectations for both of You No Strife

Prov. 3:30—Do not strive with a man without a cause, if he has done you no harm.

Prov. 17:14—The beginning of strife is like releasing water: therefore stop contention, before a quarrel starts.

Prov. 20:3—It is an honor for a man to cease from strife: but every fool will be meddling.

Phil. 2:3-Let nothing be done through selfish ambition or conceit; but in lowliness of mind let each esteem other better than himself.

James 3: 14—but if have bitter envying and strife in your hearts, glory not, and lie not against the truth.

Use Wisdom all the time and you cannot go wrong.

Prov. 4:7—Wisdom is a principal thing; therefore get wisdom: and in all thy getting get understanding.

Prov. 3:13-14 Happy is the man that finds wisdom, and the man who gains understanding: for her proceeds are better than the profits of silver, and her gain than fine gold.

Prov. 8:11-For wisdom is better than rubies; and all the things that may be desired are not to be compared to it.

How Strong is your Love?

Gen. 29:30—And Jacob served seven years for Rachel, and they seemed unto him but a few days; **for the love he had for her.**

Solomon *&:7—Many waters cannot quench love, neither can the floods drown it: if a man would give all the substance of his house for love, it would utterly be contemned.*

1 Cor. 13: 4-13

The Bible Speaks

ROMANS 12: 1-21 (KJV)

1. *Let love be without dissimulation (false **appearance**).*
2. *Abhor that which is evil.*
3. *Cleave to that which is good.*
4. *Be kindly affectionate one to another.*
5. *Give honor to one another.*
6. *Be not slothful in business.*
7. *Be fervent in spirit.*
8. *Rejoice in hope.*
9. *Be prayerful.*
10. *Be hospitable.*
11. *Bless and curse not, especially those who hurt you.*
12. *Be patient in tribulation.*
13. *Rejoice with those who rejoice.*
14. *Weep with those who weep.*
15. *Be of the same mind **(unity)**.*
16. *Be humble.*
17. *Be wise.*
18. *Do not retaliate.*
19. *Be honest.*
20. *Try to live peaceful.*
21. *Let the Lord fight for you.*
22. *Feed your enemy.*
23. *Be an **over comer, overcome evil with good**.*
24. *Have a renewed mind **(Think positively)**.*

** *If all married couples would try to live by these biblical principles their marriage would last for as long as they live. These are recommendations for both spouses alike.*

12 Ways to communicate effectively in your marriage.

1. Speak no evil one to another. James 4:11.
2. And the tongue is a fire, a world of iniquity; so is the tongue among our members, that it defiles the whole body, and sets on fire the course of nature, and it is set on fire of hell. James 3:6 Be **very careful how you use your tongue**
3. Keep thy tongue from evil, and thy lips from speaking guile Psalm 34:13.
4. Let all bitterness, and wrath and anger, and clamor, and evil speaking be put away from you, with all malice. Ephesians 4:31
5. Let no corrupt communication proceed out of your mouth, but let that which is good to the use of edifying, that it may minister grace unto the hearers. Ephesians 4:29.
6. How forcible are right words. Job 6:25.
7. A soft answer turns away wrath; but harsh words stir up anger. Proverbs 15:1
8. A hath joy by the answer of his mouth; and a word spoken in due season, how good is it. Proverbs 1
9. Pleasant words are like an honeycomb, sweet to the soul, and health to the bones. Proverbs 16:24.
10. A word fitly spoken is like apple of gold in pictures of silver. Proverbs 25:
11. Whoever guards his mouth and his tongue, keeps his soul from troubles. Prov. 21 :23.
12. A time to rend, and a time to sew: a time to keep silence, and a time to speak.Ecc.3:7.

Love According to 1 Corinthians 13

Love is patient
Love is kind
Love is not jealous
Love is not easily provoked
Love is not arrogant
Love does not act unbecomingly
Love does not seek its own
Love does not take in account wrong suffered
Love does not rejoice in unrighteousness
Love rejoices in truth
Love bears all things
Love believes all things
Love hopes all things
Love endures all things
Love never fails
Love conquers all.

Marriage Tune-up

God's view of wives

1. Submit yourself to your husband.
2. Remember you and your husband are one flesh.
3. Respect your husband.
4. Do not lie to your husband.
5. Speak your mind, but be tactful.
6. Do not allow anger to overcome you.
7. Make peace before you go to sleep (if possible)
8. Speak kind words.
9. Get rid of bitterness, wrath and strife, they will destroy you.
10. Be kind : to yourself, your spouse, your children, families and friends.
11. Be tenderhearted.
12. Be forgiving : to yourself, your husband, and others
13. Be humble.
14. Be honest: to yourself, your husband and others.
15. Be patient at all times, especially in trials.
16. Be wise: let wisdom be your teacher.
17. Be yourself: do not try to live like someone else (not a hypocrite)
18. Try to live peaceably.
19. Believe in yourself.(if you don't it is hard for others to believe in you)
20. Maintain a positive mind, and a positive attitude.
21. Learn to trust your husband.
22. Show sympathy.
23. Learn to empathize.
24. Be thoughtful.
25. Have an open mind.
26. Try to be a good house wife: Make every effort to make the home a happy place for your family. Remember that a man's home is his castle.
27. Try to make your husband happy, giving him no reason to seek happiness elsewhere.
28. Give your husband all the things that you expect to get for yourself.

God's view for Husbands

1. Love your wife as your own body.
2. You are the head of the household; therefore you must show leadership qualities.
3. Submit to your wife just as she submits to you.
4. Nourish your wife: provide for her the things that she needs, as much as it lies in your power.
5. Cherish your wife, she is as precious as rubies.
6. Your wife has become your own flesh and bones, and she should be treated as such.
7. Leave your parents and all others and cleave to your wife.
8. Do not lie to your wife.
9. Do not anger to overcome you. Learn to control your temper.
10. Do not use vulgar words to your wife: Choose your words carefully.
11. Try to encourage your wife with words that are uplifting.
12. Do not hold grudges. Let not bitterness, anger, or wrath abide in your heart.
13. Be kind to your wife at all times.
14. Be tenderhearted to your wife, she is your sweetheart.
15. Learn the art of forgiveness, and be a forgiving husband.
16. Be humble-when you are wrong admit it, and apologize.
17. Stand with your wife in every trial and tribulation.
18. Try to be a peace maker, do not make a mountain out of a mole hill.
19. Show your appreciation daily. A little 'thank you[1] can do a world of good.
20. Honor your wife, she is your queen.
21. Learn how to empathize with your wife. Be there for her: weep or laugh with her.
22. Do not love in words only, but also in deeds. Show your love daily.
23. Try to be a good house husband. Help to lessen the workload by sharing chores.
24. Make your wife your best friend: share your problems with her.
25. Take responsibility for your own actions. Passing the blame to others shows immaturity
26. Be a strong marriage builder: find ways to improve your marriage.
27. Love, love, love **your wife without limit, she should have no reason to complain.**

Look at what the Bible says

1. *Marriage is Honorable Hebrews 13:1*
2. *He that finds a wife finds a good thing ;and obtains favor from the Lord. Proverbs 18:22*
3. *Therefore shall a man leave his father and mother, and shall cleave unto his wife: and they two shall be one flesh. Genesis 2:24*
4. *Love is real. And Jacob served seven years for Rachel: And they seemed unto him but a few days/or the love he had for **her. Many waters cannot quench love; neither can the floods drown it** . . . **Songs of Solomon** 8:7 Love covers a multitude of sin. Prov.IO:12*

Check out 1 Corinthians 7

** Every man should have his own wife.

** Every woman should have her own husband.

** Neither spouse has power over their own bodies.

** You must both agree on sexual matters.

** Lack of sexual activities between spouses can lead to affairs.

QUESTIONS

1. If I had to, I would/would not marry my mate again.

2. List all the reasons that make your marriage great.

3. If you had more time, what would you do with it?

4. What are some of the things you do or say to make your spouse feel special?

5. Husbands—what percent of household chores do you share at home?

6. What amount of time do you spend with each other on hobbies or other interests?

7. Do you have a financial plan?

8. Have you any knowledge about Living Wills?

9. What are your plans for resolving conflicts?

10. Do you share your true feelings with each other?

11. Name some good characteristics of your spouse.

12. Is your sex life all that you wish it could be?

13. Is your spouse meeting your expectations?

14. Would you include your spouse in activities with your friends?

15. List some ways that your spouse has changed since you got married?

16. Do you do regular safety checks on your relationship?

17. Name some of the little things that make your marriage interesting

18. **The Little Things That Annoy Me.**

    1.   Always leaving the toilet seat up, especially at nights.

    2.   Squeezing the toothpaste tube from the middle.

    3.   Falling asleep right after making love.

    4.   Falling asleep right after eating supper.

    5.   Forgetting special dates.

    6.   Channel surfing when we watch T.V. together.

    7.   My spouse lies frequently.

    8, Frequent interruption during conversation.

    9.Failure to clean up after yourself.

Tell me how you feel.

    1.   I chose you as my partner because:

    2.   When we are together you make me feel . . .

    3.   These bad habits of yours drive me crazy:

    4.   When we are together alone, I would like you to.

    5.   It would make me happy if you would . . .

    6.   I love these outstanding qualities in you:

    7.   When we are apart it makes me feel . . .

    8.   How would you describe your spouse?

    9.   What is your idea of an ideal man/woman?

10. What are some of the things that you or your spouse could do to improve your marriage?

11. Is there anything missing from your relationship?

12. Do you participate in each others interests/hobbies?

13. How much leisure time do you and your spouse spend together?

14. What is the average number of times you compliment your mate?

15. What do you want? (for yourself, your spouse, your marriage)

16 . These are the memorable things I would like us to do again.

This is the real me.

1. My favorite foods (including fruit, vegetables, drinks, etc.)

2. These are the kinds of music I like:

3. My kind of games/sports

4. My favorite Movies/T.V. shows are:

5. The color I like best?

6. My favorite vacation spot would be?

7. These are the outdoor activities I like

8. These are the things that make me happy:

9. The kind of books I love to read?

113 Ways to spruce up your Marriage

1. Honey, you are beautiful!
2. Darling, you are handsome!
3. Sweetheart, you look gorgeous in that dress!
4. Darling, you are a wonderful wife !
5. Thank you dear for such a delicious meal e.g. Supper.
6. Wow! This place looks marvelous, thanks for your hard work dear.
7. Honey, you are a great husband.
8. Sweetheart, you are a wonderful mother to our children.
9. Honey, I like the way you help with the chores around the house.
10. Your smile brings sunshine to my life.
11. I always love to be in your company, it makes me feel special.
12. I feel so secure being with you.
13. I admire you for your kindness to me and others.
14. I love your hairstyle, it looks beautiful.
15. Thanks for being there for me when I needed you,
16. Darling, you make me feel like a queen.
17. Thank you for loving me the way that you do.
18. Sweetheart, you make me feel like a king.
19. Thank you for doing the laundry, dear.
20. I do admire you for your good qualities.
21. I love you for your courage.
22. Thank you for lifting me up when I was down.
23. Your love makes me feel special.
24. My heart belongs to you only.
25. May God bless the day we found each other.
26. We are best friends forever, it doesn't matter what happen.
27. Your kisses are hike honey.
28. Honey, you are the greatest lover in the world.
29. I always have pleasant thoughts of you.
30. I really enjoy making love to you.
31. 1 really appreciate you for your dedication,

32. Thank you for being the wind beneath my wings at times.
33. That suit makes you look like a millionaire.
34. I appreciate your honesty, darling.
35. I am glad we have each other to lean on.
36. Thank you for choosing me over the others.
37. Honey, I am sorry please forgive me.
38. Sorry dear, I was wrong 1 made a mistake . . . you were right.
39. Darling you look sensational today!
40. Honey, you make me feel magnificent.
41. You give me great satisfaction, dear.
42. Honey! I love your sense of humor.
43. Thanks for your support! Don't know how I would have made it without you.
44. Darling you are a dream come true.
45. I believe in you my dear.
46. Thank you honey for sharing in my pains.
47. Thanks for your understanding.
48. Your tenderness helps to soothe my pains.
49. The way you look at makes me feel desirable.
50. Your hugs bring comfort to me.
51. I love you!
52. I love your eyes!
53. I love your kisses!
54. I love your body!
55. You are a sweetheart!
56. Thank you for being so caring, dear.
57. Honey, you are a source of strength to me, thank you!
58. I have learned a lot from our relationship.
59. Thank you for accepting me for who I am.
60. I feel honored to be your wife.
61. I feel quite special being your husband.
62. We have been a great team together, let's keep it up.
63. . . that's interesting, t ell me more about it!
64. Darling! care for you very much !
65. Thanks for your cooperation, dear.
66. . . let's kiss and make up, honey!
67. Your smiles are comforting. They make me feel warm inside.
68. A hug a day keeps us together forever.
69. Thank you for your politeness.
70. Honey, could we please discuss this later?
71. Thanks for sharing your feelings with me.

72. Thank you for being so considerate dear.
73. Thanks for helping with the household chores.
74. Thank you for including me in decision makings.
75. Darling you are so good at what you do.
76. I am glad that you are so open-minded, honey.
77. Thanks for the efforts you put into our relationship.
78. I appreciate all the gifts you give, they make me feel wonderful.
79. Thanks for taking time out of your busy schedule to be with me.
80. Thanks for spending time with the children, it means so much to them.
81. Thanks for sharing your problems with me it makes me feel a part of you.
82. Honey! know we can make it together.
83. Honey, you are my song when I couldn't sing.
84. I admire you for your patience.
85. Darling, you are a wonderful father to our children.
86. Sweetheart, I am very proud of your accomplishments.
87. Honey, you are a hard worker, keep up the good work.
88. Wow! that perfume really turn me on dear.
89. Honey, you are always on my mind . . . you are a sweetheart.
90. Thanks dear for being honest with me about your feelings.
91. Thank you darling for being my confidant . . . it makes me feel secure!
92. Darling I appreciate you very much.
93. Oh Honey, that was a nice job you did on that . . .
94. Sweetheart, you are a great cook. I always enjoy your delicious meals.
95. Wow! you look radiant today dear.
96. Thank you for sharing everything with me darling.
97. Thank you for being so considerate dear.
98. Honey, I truly enjoy the precious moments we spend together.
99. Darling, together we are winners.

100. Thank you for your encouraging words . . . they give me strength.
101. Yes! I know you could do it.
102. Darling, I cannot find words to describe my love for you.
103. Honey, it is so good to know that you care so much.
104. Sweetheart, I know I could count on you.
105. Darling, you are sexy!
106. Well done sweetheart!
107. Honey, you are handsome!

108. You have a wonderful personality dear!
109. Thank you for your inspiration sweetheart.
110. Darling, if I had to do it again, I would still choose you.
111. Honey, you can count on me in every situation.
112. Thank you sweetheart for sharing your life with me.
113. Darling, of all the people in the world, I am happy that I have you.

60 Reasons Some Marriages Failed

1. No solid foundation to stand on.-The stronger the foundation the greater the success.
2. Lack of trust.-Without trust your relationship cannot survive life's trials.
3. Misunderstandings.-Misunderstandings lead to a lack of trust.
4. Poor communication skills.—Poor communication is as fatal in the military as in your marriage.
5. Failure to deal with current issues.-Dealing with current issues eliminates resentment.
6. Bitterness.—Bitterness is like poison to your emotions.
7. Lack of love.-Where there is no love there hatred.
8. No forgiveness.-No forgiveness, no peace in your heart.
9. No commitment.-Commitment brings stability in the marriage.
10. Incompatibility.-To succeed both of you must be on the level in your relationship.
11. Lack the desire to build a relationship.-Marriage takes two to build, not only one.
12. Immaturity.-Act like adults when dealing with issues
13. Marriage not Christ-centered.-Some started their marriage as Christians, but over the years one or both spouses changed.
14. Too many family conflicts.—Family conflicts can tear marriages apart.
15. In-law conflicts\interferences.-If the relationship is not solid and in-laws get involved, that can destroy the marriage.
16. Too much pride.-Pride will cause you to act as if you are better than your spouse; that can ruin your marriage.
17. Too busy to work on marriage.—Some people do not set priorities so they become busy with all kinds of projects which means spending less time with their spouse.
18. Greed: Material possessions take precedence over marriage.

19. Ignorance: lacking knowledge of how to really have a successful marriage.
20. Married for the wrong motives—status or money.
21. Lack of romance-no interest in your spouse.
22. Affairs.—Affairs happen for various reasons, but regardless of the reason given it will definitely cause the marriage to fail.
23. Complacency-taking each other for granted.
24. Lack of sexual relationship between you—sexual incompatibility.
25. Deceptions—habitual lying.
26. Hypocrisy-One partner being a great pretender.
27. Lack of planning.—It is amazing how much planning is put into sending astronauts to the space station yet for our own marriage we fail to make plans for success.
28. Abuses: drug, physical, verbal, sexual.
29. Lack of respect for each other.—with no respect in the marriage there will no care for your spouse.
30. Cultural barriers. When couples married in different cultures without good understanding of the cultures it can cause problems.
31. Selfishness.-Many people find it difficult to share with others based on their background; therefore they find it hard to change their selfishness even though they are married.
32. Marital discords.
33. Anger.
34. Loneliness
35. Inconsistencies.
36. Pessimism.
37. Dishonesty.
38. Passivity,
39. Disagreements.
40. Stubbornness.
41. Negative attitudes.
42. Low self-esteem.
43. Lack of wisdom.
44. Alcoholism.
45. Fail to reconcile differences.
46. Loss of interest in spouse.
47. Failure to compromise.
48. Unhappiness.
49. Husband failed to fulfill his role as head of the household.
50. Wife failed in her household duties.
51. Lack of motivation to make marriage succeed.

52. Unwilling to seek profession help.
53. Negligent to build on foundations.
54. Change of values.
55. No sense of direction in marriage.
56. No affection between you.
57. Lost sight of marriage vows.
58. Expectations not met.
59. Unwilling to adapt to any form of changes.
60. The union got damaged by years of neglect.

MARRIAGE REVIEW

1. If I had to, I would/would not marry my mate again.
2. List some of the reasons you think your marriage is successful/not successful.
3. What are some of the things that you would consider a blessing in your marriage?
4. What would you do if you had more free time?
5. What are some of the things you say or do to make your spouse special?
6. Husbands-what percent of household chores do you do around the house?
7. On average, how much time do you spend with each other?
8. How do you normally resolve conflicts between you?
9. Do you share your feelings with each other when you are hurt?
10. Name some good characteristics of your spouse.
11. Is your sex life all that you wish it to be? Yes ( ) No ( )
12. Are you always honest about your sexual feelings? e.g. Would you tell your spouse if you are not being satisfied?
13. Name some of the changes you have seen in your spouse since you got married.
14. Do you do regular safety checks on your marriage ?
15. When I am hurt the first person I tell is: My best friend, my parents, my spouse, no one.
16. We both equally share the responsibilities of childrearing Yes ( ) No ( )
17. My spouse is my best friend yes ( ) No ( )
18. The relationship between my spouse and me is: Great ( ) Not so great ( )

MARRIAGE TUNE-UP

FOR A MARRIAGE TO GROW AND DEVELOP WELL IT NEEDS:

1. Love.
2. Trust.
3. Respect.
4. Commitment.
5. Romance.
6. Friendship.
7. Understanding.
8. Good communication skills.
9. Good listening skills.
10. Creativity.
11. Flexibility.
12. A good sense of humor.
13. To say "I LOVE YOU" frequently.
14. Forgiveness.
15. Good support for each other.
16. Positive attitude.
17. To be best friends.
18. Adaptability.
19. Honesty.
20. To be realistic.
21. Kindness.
22. Self-confidence.
23. Wisdom.
24. Thoughtfulness.
25. Tender Loving Care.
26. Regular tuning.
27. Sex.
28. Good planning.
29. To be nurtured.
30. Compatibility.
31. A good foundation.

YOUR MARRIAGE IS TUNED AND READY TO SUCCEED:

1. When your love for each other is as sound as the love you have for yourself. The reality is that if we do not love our selves we cannot truly love some one else. This is one of the problems with many marriages. Some people go into marriage trying to give something that they themselves do not have-love.

2. When your line of communication is firmly connected and free from all static. Communication is our life line; we cannot survive without some forms of communication. You must learn to communicate effectively with your spouse if you want to have a happy marriage.

3. When you have a high level of respect for each other. As a couple neither of you should lose respect for the other. Try to live an up standing life to earn the respect of your spouse.

4. When Lovemaking is pleasurable to both of you (no faking orgasm) Work hard to keep the love making as pleasurable as can be by making sex fun.

5. When your relationship has reached the comfort zone, where you know that you can share all secrets with your spouse without fear of being judged.

6. When your understanding has made it to the point of knowing when to laugh and when to cry with each other. When you understand your spouse there will be no need to tress about things that may happen in your marriage.

7. When you can trust each other without the shadow of a doubt. Trust helps to build confidence in your marriage.

8. When both of you share the same level of happiness all the time. It does not worth your time and effort if you are in a relationship and you are not happy. Therefore, if there is unhappiness you need to examine the relationship and try to fix the problem.

9. When you feel the connection of oneness between you; and you know you can rely on each other for support. Like a link in a chain you need your spouse to make the marriage work well. That is the reason it is so important that you make that connection.

   Neither of you feel neglected by your spouse. We can get too busy with various activities in life to the point where we put others or other things before our spouse. Your spouse should not have to feel neglected to the point of seeking others for comfort.

10. When you give gifts to each other just to say "I Love You". To keep your love alive in the marriage it is good to practice giving gifts. Maybe just a small thing as a chocolate bar will allow your spouse to know that you care.

11. When you do not have to backbite your spouse. It is very important to remember to do unto your spouse as you would like your spouse to do unto you. When something goes wrong between you and your spouse and you find it difficult to talk face to face, try writing a note or a letter to express your feelings.

12. When you can resolve your conflicts maturely. This will take a long time to accomplish but with practice it will happen over time.

13. When you can take responsibility for your own actions and behaviors. It is in our nature to blame others when something goes wrong; however, you should learn to take responsibility for your own actions and many conflicts will be resolved.

14. When you can work together as a team to accomplish any task. Working together as a team will help your marriage to conquer difficult tasks.

15. When you do not have to compete with your spouse for affection. A sign of maturity in the marriage is when you know who you are as a person. This allows you to give yourself freely to love and to be loved. You love yourself first so you don't have to feel left out if no one loves you.

16. When your spouse is your best friend. This should be the first step in any marriage. The couple should seek to be best of friends because that brings with it a certain amount of closeness. True friendship is not easily broken.

17. When you can accept each other with all faults and failures. We often say 'no one is perfect' which is true. For your love to grow and mature in your marriage you must love unconditionally.

18. When you work together to reach planned goals. You and your spouse must keep the same focus or your goals in life will not be reached.

19. When you find you cannot stay away from each other for too long. Love is like a magnet it draws people together. Your marriage is well tuned when you find it hard to stay away from your spouse. When you are apart you think about your spouse a lot and you can't wait for you to be together again.

Planning
for
a

Successful
Marriage

So You Want To Get Married ?

Marriage is honorable. God's desire for marriage is that couples who are joined together in holy matrimony, have a happy and successful marriage.

Marriage is a great responsibility, and only those who are serious about God's plan for marriage should enter therein. Anyone considering marriage must be willing to spend time in planning and preparation to make it succeed. It is recommended that those considering marriage study the successful marriages of others, and learn the secrets of their success.

Marriage is said to be an institution: a place where two individuals from various backgrounds come together as one flesh. When a couple gets married, a new world of learning begins. All the things that you knew about each other during courtship seem to be forgotten, and both of you have to begin to learn about each other again. Marriage is a personal learning experience. Textbook can only prepare you, but you have to experience it to understand it.

It is very important that you prepare well for marriage. This means knowing yourself as well as knowing the kind of partner you would like to marry. You must know what you want even before courtship begins. That is the reason you date. You want to make sure that you find the kind of person that will be compatible for you. Dating could take a long time before you actually decide to move into courtship. Courtship is that period of time that you decide that you need to get to know more about each other, as you make a decision for marriage. During courtship you should learn about each other's anger, bad habits, temperaments, patience, good and bad qualities, as well as each other's strengths and weaknesses. You should try to learn about each other's feelings and try to understand how to deal with each other. The preparation and planning for marriage cannot be over emphasized, because marriage is for a lifetime, and only with proper planning and a strong love for each other will you be able to succeed when the trials of life come upon you. You should also note that marriage is not a fairytale. There is no "living happily ever after" without lots of hard work. And that hard work must begin long before you get married.

So if you really want to get married you must count the cost. You are both responsible to make 100 per cent preparation if you are 100 per cent sure that you want to have a happy and successful marriage. You can have a wonderful marriage, but it all depend on how much time you put in it to make it work.

COURTSHIP

Courtship is a time of connection between you and the person you intend to marry. It is a time when there will be more questions than answers from both parties involved. Courtship is a time of getting to know each other. During this time both of you will seek to lay a foundation on which to build your marriage It is very important that you be honest to each other as you develop your relationship. Do not assume anything; get the facts from your mate. The only way to get the facts is to ask questions. Do not be afraid to ask questions, especially about things that you believe would affect your marriage. Many marriages ended in divorce because some people failed to ask pertinent questions during courtship.

People who are getting married must have a good knowledge of each other. By dating and talking to each other many things will be disclosed to you, that will help you to determine your future. There must be a good line of communication between you from the beginning. This is important to allow freedom of information between you. The word here is talk, talk, talk. Talk about your feelings, your families, your friends, your hobbies, your interests, your likes and dislikes. Talk about anything that you believe will help to improve your relationship. Be wise and observant, and listen carefully as you talk. Listen to the way your mate talks about others: family members, friends, and employers. The way your mate talks about others will give you an idea of what will be said about you behind your back.

As courtship progressed both of you must seek to understand each other. Be real, put away falsehood, because whatever you try to cover up now will come to light eventually. Do not use profane or abusive language to each other At the first sign of any kind of abuse, the line should be drawn. Be up front and let your mate know that you do not appreciate being abused. Do not be naive. People who are naive usually end up getting hurt. Do not take anything for granted. Courtship is the time to deal with all the "little insignificant" issues. If you do not deal with them during courtship they will come back to harm you in your marriage.

Do not sell yourself short

In marriage as in all aspect of life, you need to be the best you can. You must prepare yourself for marriage just as you prepare yourself for that important job. Many people spent years in College or university to prepare for a career, yet never try to prepare for marriage. As you prepare for marriage, you must take time to know yourself. Know who you are: know your strengths and weaknesses, know what you want to achieve in life and work hard for it. Be honest to yourself and do not sell yourself short. Be confident in yourself. Do not be content with less than the best. Aim high and follow your dreams, even as you choose your marriage partner. Be knowledgeable: read many books on various subjects, read magazines, and newspapers. Study hard, take courses of different interests. If you are unsure about something, research it. Write down your goals, set a time to achieve them, and work hard to obtain them. Seek to be mature and independent. When you are independent no one can take disadvantage of you. Many people have been hurt by others whom they have depended on. Think positive and maintain an open mind. Have a positive attitude and stand up for what is right. Having confidence in yourself will empower you to make right choices in life.

How Do I Know If I Am Right

Marriage is not a business of trial and error; it is a lifetime investment in someone you love. As you plan for marriage there will be many tests and trials that will either build or destroy your relationship. Do not be afraid of the trials that you will encounter during courtship; they are indicators for your marriage

When it seems as if you are not on the right track, and you are having doubts about your mate; take a piece of paper and write down all the advantages and disadvantages, in marrying the person you are now dating. Look at the result and use that as your guide. If you discover that your expectations are not being met, then you need to discuss it with your mate.

As you continue in courtship, let the love that attracted you to each other from the beginning continue to guide. You must feel that strong bond between you, and you must know without the shadow of a doubt that this relationship is good for both of you.

No relationship can or will ever grow successfully on falsehood or deception. Both of you must talk honestly about your feelings. There should be no deep secret between you and the person you are going to marry.

A Solid Foundation

A solid foundation is the strength of every successful marriage. Every strong building has a solid foundation and every strong tree has deep roots. Nature teaches that trees that survived storms and hurricanes have strong deep roots. This same principle applies to all good marriages. Here are some materials on which to lay the foundation for a successful marriage.

LOVE: Build on love and your marriage will withstand the storms of life. Love is the glue that cements your relationship. Without love it is impossible to have a good, long lasting marriage.

TRUST: You must trust each other in all situations regardless of the circumstances. Trust means total commitment to each other.

FRIENDSHIP: Marriage is more than being husband and wife.lt means being a friend to each other. A friend is one who will be there with you at all times. A friend knows everything about you, yet loves you as you are. No one can come between you.

RESPECT: Respect is earned not demanded.lt is contagious and will help you to smooth your relationship.

WISDOM: Wisdom is a precious gem that no marriage can survive without. Use lots of wisdom especially in difficult times.

UNDERSTANDING: Let understanding guide you through those spots in your marriage. You must be willing to put yourself in your mate's place at times when dealing with problems.

KINDNESS: Kindness must come from the heart. It must be used daily without measure to overcome the obstacles in your relationship. Kindness means going a second mile for your mate.

FORGIVENESS: Forgiveness is important for every successful marriage. It takes lots of practice to learn to forgive, but it will help to keep your relationship in tact. If you expect to be forgiven you must first learn to forgive.

HONESTY: You must first be honest to yourself and it will become a part of your daily life in marriage.

INTEGRITY: Try to maintain integrity in your life at all times and your marriage will develop strength. You and your words must stand in all tests.

PARTNERSHIP: Partnership is both of you working together on the same goals in the thick and the thin.

COMMUNICATION: Communication is the vital sign of a healthy marriage. It will take hard work, but a good line of communication will produce happiness in marriage. Try to keep your communication lines free from erosion, damage or being cut. Your marriage has a better chance of survival when communication is in tact.

LOYALTY: Loyalty means two people committing themselves to each other to share all their dreams and aspirations. You must stick together in all kinds of weather.

THOUGHTFULNESS: Your mate is a part of you and should be in your thoughts at all times. You must both look out for each other's interests. Thinking about each other will lessen the chance of hurting each other's feelings.

AMBITION: When you are ambitious you will work hard to make your life and your marriage succeed.

INTELLIGENCE: Your intelligence should help you through those turbulent times in your marriage. Keep on learning.

CREATIVITY: Being creative is a way of helping to get boredom out of your marriage. You should develop various ways to make each other happy.

HUMILITY: Humility will make it easier for you to forgive and to accept forgiveness. Try to maintain a humble spirit at all times.

SELF-CONFIDENCE: Know yourself. Be proud of who you are, and know what you want out of life. Work hard to attain your goals.

SELF-ESTEEM: Do not put yourself down, neither allow anyone to put you down. Think positively about yourself. You are as precious as everyone else. Count your blessings and maintain a positive attitude about life.

You can add other good materials to your foundation as you seek to build a strong marriage, one that will be able to stand when the big storms hit you and your marriage.

100 Percent and Nothing less

Like every strong tower, your marriage requires 100 percent support from each of you, in order to conquer the battles of life. It will take the best effort from both of you to make your marriage succeed. Your whole mind, body and spirit must be committed to make your marriage work. Remember that you will get out only what you put in; therefore it is important that you give 100 percent at all times to make it succeed.

Bad Habits

Bad habits can become a problem in marriage if it is not dealt with at an early stage in courtship. Do not ignore bad habits thinking that they will go away after you are married. Try to talk about them from the beginning and see if both of you can work out a solution before marriage. Some bad habits may take a long time to get rid of, so you must be willing to exercise patience and understanding with your mate.

Words Are Powerful

Words are not just mere wind they are powerful vehicles that can be very damaging to those who receive them. Listen to how you talk to each other, and try to use kind words at all times. Do not at anytime use profane or derogatory language to each other. Verbal abuse is wrong and none of you should resort to it at anytime. Think before you speak, even when you are angry. Think positive and build a positive relationship by using words that are pleasant, encouraging and uplifting.

Jealousy

Jealousy is a sign of insecurity, and if it is left unattended it can destroy your relationship with others, including your mate. Watch for signs of jealousy and try to correct it before marriage. Try to find the root of the jealousy, whether it is from you or your mate, and try to eradicate it. If you find that you cannot trust your partner during courtship, it will be difficult to trust him/her in marriage. You and your mate need to seek professional help before you get married, because it will only get worse if you wait until after marriage.

Nagging

Nagging is not a word that many people want to talk about, but it does exist in some marriages. Nagging is usually not done intentionally; however, it can damage the relationship between you and your mate. The best way to avoid nagging is to get to know your partner well. Try to study your partner's temperament, and know when it is safe to discuss certain issues. Timing is important when making confrontation. Use wisdom, patience and understanding, and try different approach to deal with issues. Try to avoid conflict at all times.

Compromise

As you make plans for marriage, do not forget that both of you will be bringing your own individuality in the marriage. In order for the marriage to maintain equilibrium, each of you must learn the art of compromise. When you make decisions always leave room for negotiation. You need to know that there is a difference between negotiation and manipulation, learn the difference. When you compromise, both of you may have to give up certain rights in order to achieve a peaceful resolution. Giving up your rights should not be seen as a failure. Remember, you don't always have to be right. If you make a mistake or you are wrong about something, admit it, apologize and move on. Sure, it is not easy for some people to apologize, but lots of practice will make it look easy.

Making Plans

For fear of disappointment, many people do not like to make plans. While there are others who find it very important to make plans for everything. As a couple you need to make plans together, especially major plans that concern both of you. When your mate knows what you are doing, there will be no need for speculations or assumptions. Planning together will eliminate division between you and you mate, because both of you will know exactly what is happening in each other's life. When you plan together it will help you to understand the goals you both want to attain.It will also help you to overcome difficult obstacles in your lives.

Planned Parenthood

Children are precious; however, not all married couples want children. On the other hand, some couples want to have many children, while others only want one or two. During courtship you both need to establish your true feelings about children. Do not assume anything, get the facts from your mate. Talk about the number of children both of you would like to have. Then decide on the number of children both of you can afford to support financially.

There is a lot more to parenthood than just biological connections. It takes careful planning and full support from both parents. As you think about marriage and children, it would be advisable to consider these simple guidelines:

1. Think about the couple's needs—Are we ready for a baby?
2. Think about the child's needs—how much time and effort can we afford to give the child now?
3. Coping mechanism: What kind of resources do we have to help us cope with the baby?
4. What about baby sitting?-Who will care for the baby?
5. Working parents: Should one of us stay home to care for the child? Are we financially able to have a stay-at-home parent?
6. Responsibilities: How are we going to share the responsibilities? Does the husband have any knowledge of the duties involved with caring for a baby?
7. The number and sex of children should be discussed, e.g. we would like to have two children of the opposite sex, or two children of the same sex.

Culture plays an important role when planning for parenthood. In some cultures it is customary to have large families, while in others it is very significant that a male child be born in the family. These and other factors can cause problems in marriage if they are not dealt with during courtship. It is imperative that both of you know what to expect; and plan for it. The message: **Do not take anything for granted, always try to get the facts; your marriage will work out much better.**

Birth Control

Birth control must be a part of your discussion during courtship. This is a concern for both of you, and should not be left up to the wife alone. The both of you must take the time to study the different methods of birth control, and try to learn the side effects, and the effectiveness of each method. After you complete your research and decide on the one you would like to use, you must discuss it with your family doctor.

There are people who do not believe in family planning; there are others who cannot use any of the methods that are available. Everyone is different; every couple must decide what is best for them. However, whatever decisions made must be joint decisions that will bring happiness to both of you.

Pregnancy

Pregnancy is not a subject that is usually discussed during courtship, but it cannot be ignored, especially if it something you are looking forward to anxiously. Pregnancy is usually a joyful experience for married couples, but it is important to let you know that this could also be a stressful time for some expected parents.

During pregnancy there may be lots of mood swings, and slow days, so the line of communication must be very good in order to make it through those rough spots. This is the time when you both need to make extra effort to support each other in: love, patience and understanding. Talk to each other about your feelings. Do a lot of reading together, talk to friends, and attend parenting classes in preparation for the new baby.

Tips For When The Baby Arrives

It may not be obvious to many people, but many new parents are very scared when their new baby arrives. Ignorance may be the cause of many fears, and that is the reason it is so important to have a broad knowledge on child bearing before the baby arrives. Here are some things you should know as you plan for the arrival of your baby.

1. There will be some tiresome days and nights as you both care for the child. You must be sensitive to each other's needs and feelings. You must support each other in everything; showing much patience, love and understanding all the time.
2. There will be fatigue, stress, loneliness, jealousy, feelings of isolation, lack of sex, feelings of rejection, feelings of inadequacy, along with

all kinds of other mixed emotions. As both of you encounter these feelings you must learn how to deal with them so that none of you will get hurt while trying to give your baby the best care.

3. The responsibilities of childrearing must be shared by both parents. Both of you must work as a team to care for the baby. Every husband must learn to be a good father. Many men leave all or most of the responsibilities of child rearing to the mother, but that should not happen at all.

4. Young babies can be difficult to deal with; therefore you should prepare yourself adequately. You will need lots of patience to deal with the unexpected circumstances. There will be sleepless nights and difficult days to encounter from time to time as you care for your new baby. Try **to get all the help you can so that you can be the best parents in the world, and yet remain the most loving and dearest couple of all.**

5. A new baby can really be a challenge and a true test of your relationship. Use lots of love, wisdom, and understanding to overcome the challenges.

Conflicts

Conflicts are the inevitable of every marriage. They can occur at anytime and anywhere. Conflicts come sometimes due to misunderstandings, as well as from other factors. During courtship many people will hide their true self; not wanting to 'hurt* their partner's feelings they reserve many things until after marriage.It is not a matter of whether conflicts will come, it is how they are dealt with when they occur that will determine the success of your marriage. Here are some tips that may be helpful in resolving conflicts in your marriage.

1. Learn to control your temper. Never yell at each other. Try to speak softly even when you are angry. Proverbs 15:1 says "A soft answer turns away wrath, but harsh words stir up anger."

2. Study the mood of your spouse and know when to discuss certain issues.

3. Use wisdom when making confrontations.

4. Think out the situation before you act or say something you may regret.

5. Sometimes you may have to swallow your pride and eat your words to have a peaceful resolution.

6. Put yourself in your partner's place and see how it would feel if you were on the other side of the conflict. Some people like to give insults that they themselves cannot handle.

7. Get the facts. Do not assume anything because that can lead to conflicts. If you are not sure about something ask your mate to explain it.

8. Learn to apologize when you make mistakes. Many conflicts remain unresolved due to pride. Remember that no one is infallible, we all make mistakes. The sooner you apologize, the sooner the conflicts will be resolved.

You and Religion

Religion is a significant part of many people's life; therefore it should be discussed during courtship. Learn all you can about each other's religious back ground, and see if it would affect you in your marriage. As you plan, be concerned about your wedding, the blessing of your children, the school your children attend, and other religious activities you may want to get involved in later on in life.

Money, Money, Money

Money is a big subject in all marriages, and it must not be taken lightly in courtship. Honesty, good communication, and proper planning should help you deal with financial issues. Use wisdom, patience, and understanding to overcome any financial problems. Always have a workable plan that is suitable to your budget. Try to live within your means. Make short-term and long-term goals and stick to them. You should decide on major purchases. It does not matter what happen, do not allow money to destroy your marriage. When something goes wrong try to talk about as mature people. Let there be no secrets between you, it will ruin your marriage. Use your money wisely.

Sex, as designed by God, is a special part of marriage; yet it is usually one of the least discussed topics in many marriages. Right from the beginning of courtship the communication lines must be open in regard to sex. Every person who has a desire to be married should make the effort to be educated in all aspect of sexual issues. It is very important that you prepare yourself to be the best sex partner your spouse will ever have. When each of you go into marriage with the desire to be the best, it will become easy for both of you to enjoy each other's company, and your marriage will succeed without much effort.

You both need to learn the art of lovemaking, because you are equally responsible to give pleasure to each other. You do not have to get into pornography to learn about sex, there are lots of other good materials that will guide you. The reason there are so many problems with sex in marriages is the fact that many couples are dishonest. You are being dishonest to yourself when you fail to disclose your true feelings to your mate. If you tell your spouse that you are "O.K." when you are not, you are not only lying to your spouse; you are deceiving yourself. For many people it seems easier to do sex than to talk about it. For sex to succeed in any marriage both partners must be able to talk about it: intelligently, openly, and wisely. Do not assume, get the facts from each other. There are many reasons some couples find sex a turn-off, and lost the desire in what should be a very enjoyable part of their physical life.

Here are some sexual turn-offs and mood spoilers to avoid on your way to a wonderful sex life.

1. Feelings: being hurt (emotionally) by spouse. It is difficult to make love when there is hurt feelings. You both need to try to get rid of any hurt feelings, and get back on good terms before attempting to make love.
2. Poor body odor (no perfume) is a definite turn-off. This may seem trivial, but there has been lots of complains about this. You should try to be your best for your spouse at all times. Keep your body odor under control by using nice perfume, especially perfume that you know your mate likes.
3. Bad breath (teeth not brushed). It is a good practice to keep your breath fresh at all times.
4. Dirty, smelly, sweaty clothes and socks are also turn-offs. Keep a constant check on these areas, and do let them spoil the mood.
5. Physical appearance. Try to look lovely for each other always, so that you can attract your mate. It is very important that both of you watch your diets so that you do not put on too much weight. There has been lots of complains from husbands and wives whose spouse has gained excess weight after marriage. This has affected their marriage in many

ways, especially sexually. Try to do everything possible to show your spouse that you are the most desirable person in the whole world, and you want to keep it that way always.

6. Fatigue: When it comes to sex, wives usually complain about being fatigued, especially if they have to be a worker, a mother, a wife, and do other things around the house. They feel fatigued when they have to do all the house work, with no help from the husband, and still expected to be available for sex whenever her husband is ready for it.

7. Unkempt hair and beard can be a turn-off for some wives, and that has kept them away from wanting to have sex.

8. Lack of timing can also be a turn-off from sex. You should try to use wisdom and good communication at all time when dealing with sex. Think and use your time wisely, it will make sex so much more enjoyable.

9. Lack of romance is a sexual turn-off too. Many couples sex life died due to lack of romance. Both of you must seek to maintain romance in themarriage. Try hard to remember the sparks that brought you together from the beginning and use it to keep the fire burning in your marriage.

10. Boredom due to lack of creativity, can be a big turn-off in your sex life. Being creative will help you to have fun in your sex life.

Life Insurance

It is essential that you both have a good life insurance. Life is unpredictable, so to ease the financial burden of loved ones left behind, get an insurance.

Will

In the best interest of your loved ones it is advisable to make a Will. Anyone at any age can make a Will, it is not only for senior citizens.

www.ingramcontent.com/pod-product-compliance
Lightning Source LLC
Chambersburg PA
CBHW021243280526
45784CB00005B/2218